EUROPEAN COUNTRIES TODAY
GREECE

EUROPEAN COUNTRIES TODAY
TITLES IN THE SERIES

Austria	Italy
Belgium	Netherlands
Czech Republic	Poland
Denmark	Portugal
France	Spain
Germany	Sweden
Greece	United Kingdom
Ireland	European Union Facts & Figures

EUROPEAN COUNTRIES TODAY
GREECE

Dominic J. Ainsley

MASON CREST

Mason Crest
450 Parkway Drive, Suite D
Broomall, Pennsylvania PA 19008
(866) MCP-BOOK (toll free)

Copyright © 2019 by Mason Crest, an imprint of National Highlights, Inc. All rights reserved. No part of this publication may be reproduced or transmitted in any form or by any means, electronic or mechanical, including photocopying, recording, taping, or any information storage and retrieval system, without permission in writing from the publisher.

First printing
9 8 7 6 5 4 3 2 1

ISBN: 978-1-4222-3985-8
Series ISBN: 978-4222-3977-3
ebook ISBN: 978-1-4222-7800-0

Library of Congress Cataloging-in-Publication Data

Names: Ainsley, Dominic J., author.
Title: Greece / Dominic J. Ainsley.
Description: Broomall, Pennsylvania : Mason Crest, 2019. | Series: European countries today | Includes index.
Identifiers: LCCN 2018007577 (print) | LCCN 2018016015 (ebook) | ISBN 9781422278000 (eBook) | ISBN 9781422239858 (hardback)
Subjects: LCSH: Greece--Juvenile literature.
Classification: LCC DF717 (ebook) | LCC DF717 .A66 2019 (print) | DDC 949.5--dc23
LC record available at https://lccn.loc.gov/2018007577

Printed in the United States of America

Cover images
Main: *The Greek ruins at Delphi.*
Left: *Greek produce including Feta, olives, and rosemary.*
Center: *Dancers in traditional dress.*
Right: *The famous blue and white buildings of Santorini.*

QR CODES AND LINKS TO THIRD-PARTY CONTENT

You may gain access to certain third-party content ("Third- Party Sites") by scanning and using the QR Codes that appear in this publication (the "QR Codes"). We do not operate or control in any respect any information, products, or services on such Third-Party Sites linked to by us via the QR Codes included in this publication, and we assume no responsibility for any materials you may access using the QR Codes. Your use of the QR Codes may be subject to terms, limitations, or restrictions set forth in the applicable terms of use or otherwise established by the owners of the Third-Party Sites. Our linking to such Third-Party Sites via the QR Codes does not imply an endorsement or sponsorship of such Third-Party Sites or the information, products, or services offered on or through the Third-Party Sites, nor does it imply an endorsement or sponsorship of this publication by the owners of such Third-Party Sites.

CONTENTS

Greece at a Glance	6
Chapter 1: Greece's Geography & Landscape	11
Chapter 2: The Government & History of Greece	25
Chapter 3: The Greek Economy	43
Chapter 4: Citizens of Greece: People, Customs & Culture	55
Chapter 5: The Famous Cities of Greece	69
Chapter 6: A Bright Future for Greece	85
Chronology	90
Further Reading & Internet Resources	91
Index	92
Picture Credits & Author	96

KEY ICONS TO LOOK FOR:

Words to Understand: These words with their easy-to-understand definitions will increase the reader's understanding of the text while building vocabulary skills.

Sidebars: This boxed material within the main text allows readers to build knowledge, gain insights, explore possibilities, and broaden their perspectives by weaving together additional information to provide realistic and holistic perspectives.

Educational Videos: Readers can view videos by scanning our QR codes, providing them with additional content to supplement the text. Examples include news coverage, moments in history, speeches, iconic sports moments, and much more!

Text-Dependent Questions: These questions send the reader back to the text for more careful attention to the evidence presented there.

Research Projects: Readers are pointed toward areas of further inquiry connected to each chapter. Suggestions are provided for projects that encourage deeper research and analysis.

GREECE AT A GLANCE

MAP OF EUROPE

The Geography of Greece

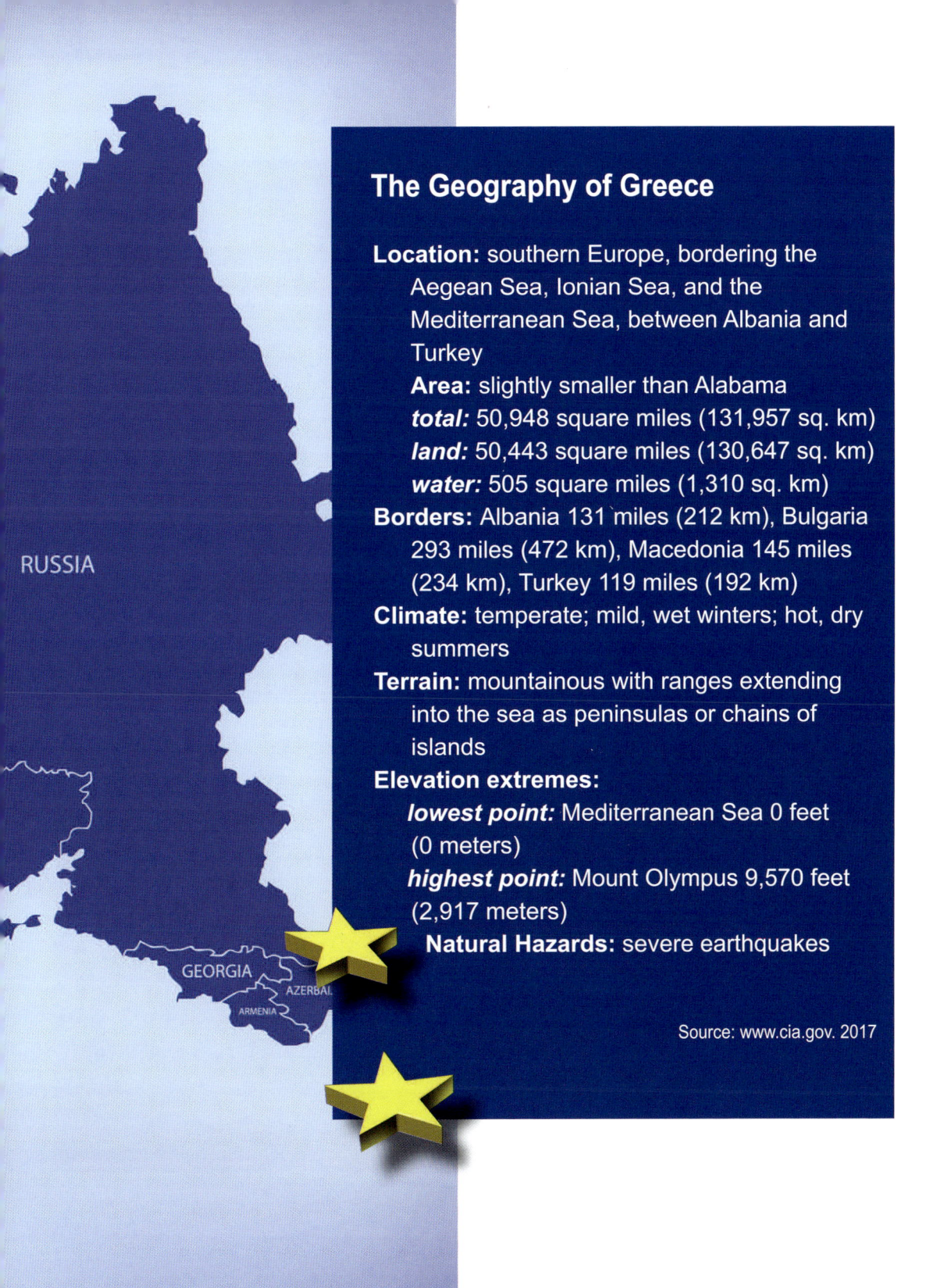

Location: southern Europe, bordering the Aegean Sea, Ionian Sea, and the Mediterranean Sea, between Albania and Turkey
Area: slightly smaller than Alabama
total: 50,948 square miles (131,957 sq. km)
land: 50,443 square miles (130,647 sq. km)
water: 505 square miles (1,310 sq. km)
Borders: Albania 131 miles (212 km), Bulgaria 293 miles (472 km), Macedonia 145 miles (234 km), Turkey 119 miles (192 km)
Climate: temperate; mild, wet winters; hot, dry summers
Terrain: mountainous with ranges extending into the sea as peninsulas or chains of islands
Elevation extremes:
lowest point: Mediterranean Sea 0 feet (0 meters)
highest point: Mount Olympus 9,570 feet (2,917 meters)
Natural Hazards: severe earthquakes

Source: www.cia.gov. 2017

GREECE AT A GLANCE

Flag of Greece

Greece has a mainland area extending into the Mediterranean Sea and around 2,000 islands, mainly in the Aegean Sea. Greece has been ruled by the Romans and the Turks over the centuries, but finally became independent in the early nineteenth century. At one time, the flag was a single blue cross, but this has since given way to the present flag. The cross represents Christianity and blue and white are the national colors of Greece, the blue for the sea and sky and white for the purity of the freedom fighters who established Greece's independence.

ABOVE: A traditional taverna in Larissa. Greece's favorable climate means that customers can dine outside for many months of the year.

EUROPEAN COUNTRIES TODAY: GREECE

The People of Greece

Population: 10,768,477 (July 2017 est.)
Ethnic Groups: Greek 93%, other (foreign citizens) 7%
note: data represent citizenship, since Greece does not collect data on ethnicity
Age Structure:
   0–14 years: 13.83%
   15–24 years: 9.67%
   25–54 years: 42.45%
   55–64 years: 13.13%
   65 years and over: 20.91%
Population Growth Rate: -0.06% (2017 est.)
Birth Rate: 8.4 births/1,000 population (2017 est.)
Death Rate: 11.3 deaths/1,000 population (2017 est.)
Migration Rate: 2.3 migrant(s)/1,000 population (2017 est.)
Infant Mortality Rate: 4.6 deaths/1,000 live births
Life Expectancy at Birth:
   Total population: 80.7 years
   Male: 78 years
   Female: 83.4 years (2017 est.)
Total Fertility Rate: 1.43 children born/woman (2017 est.)
Religions: Greek Orthodox (official) 98%, Muslim 1.3%, other 0.7%
Languages: Greek (official) 99%, other (includes English and French) 1%
Literacy Rate: 97.7%

Source: www.cia.gov 2017

Words to Understand

maritime: Relating to, or bordering on, the sea.

mythology: The myths of a particular group or culture.

navigable: Deep enough and wide enough to afford passage to ships.

Chapter One
GREECE'S GEOGRAPHY & LANDSCAPE

Greece is often considered the cradle of Western civilization. Its forms of government, art, and literature have provided the foundation for the advancements of later nations and cultures. Things such as city-states, Homer's *The Odyssey*, and Socrates come to mind when Greece is mentioned. However, it is also a modern country, making use of new technology and providing its people with comfortable living standards.

Greece, or the Hellenic Republic as it is officially known, is located on the southern portion of the Balkan Peninsula and also includes the Peloponnesian Peninsula. The present-day country has an area of 50,948 square miles (131,957 square kilometers), roughly the size of the state of Alabama.

The Terrain: Coastlines to Mountains

Since Greece is located on the Balkan Peninsula, the ocean surrounds it on three sides. The Aegean, Ionian, and Mediterranean seas form 8,498 miles (13,676 kilometers) of coastline stretching around the country. Greece's land boundary with other nations is only 689 miles (1,110 kilometers) long. This strategic location on the water has ruled the lives of the Greek people for all of its history, aiding in trade, military pursuits, and food transportation.

The land that makes up Greece is extremely mountainous. The Pindus Mountains, which stretch from north to south, dominate the center of the peninsula. Much of the land is dry and very rocky, although the west has several lakes, and about 28 percent of the land is suitable for agriculture. Mountains cover over four-fifths of Greece's land, and much of the terrain is 4,920 feet (1,500 meters) above sea level. The highest mountain in the nation is the famed Mount Olympus, which is 9,570 feet (2,917 meters) high.

GREECE'S GEOGRAPHY & LANDSCAPE

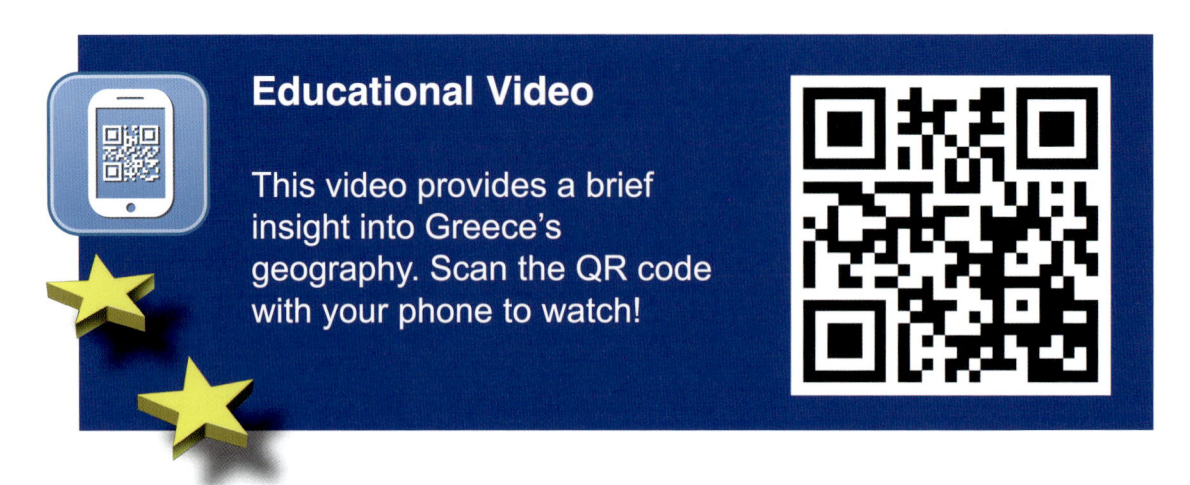

Educational Video

This video provides a brief insight into Greece's geography. Scan the QR code with your phone to watch!

ABOVE: *The southern side of Mount Olympus. According to Greek mythology, the mountain was home to the gods and godesses.*

12

EUROPEAN COUNTRIES TODAY: GREECE

The geographical position of Greece in the ancient world was probably a crucial factor in the development of its richly varied **mythology**, which absorbed elements from a number of different cultures. Because Greece lies towards the eastern end of the Mediterranean, it is a stepping stone between west and east, between Europe and western Asia; groups of islands in the Aegean form a bridge between Greece and Asia Minor, and the landmass itself stretches southwards into the Mediterranean basin toward Egypt and Libya.

Four-fifths of Greece is mountainous, or semi-mountainous, but from the mountains the sea is usually visible. From early times, the rugged nature of the terrain encouraged its inhabitants to travel more easily by sailing round the

ABOVE: *The island of Symi, which forms part of the Dodecanese island group, is in the southern Aegean Sea.*

GREECE'S GEOGRAPHY & LANDSCAPE

Olive

Greece is famous for its ancient olive trees, some of them as old as two thousand years. The indigenous olive tree (wild olive tree) first appeared in the eastern Mediterranean, but it was in Greece that it was first cultivated. Since then, it has been part of the traditions and the culture of the Greek people. Homer (the Greek poet) describe olive oil as "liquid gold," referring to its properties in cooking, medicine, and skin care. Throughout the centuries, the olive tree has been given a special status and is considered a symbol of peace, abundance, and great natural power.

coast and from the mainland to nearby islands and other Mediterranean coastal areas. The deeply indented coastline, sheltered bays, gulfs, and archipelagoes, together with the tideless Mediterranean and unusually clear light made sea travel comparatively easy, so trade and cultural contacts with nearby **maritime** civilizations were established early on.

Yet the cultural diversity that such contact brought to Greece was balanced by an intense and proud localism largely caused by the nature of the land itself. Since agriculture was by far the most important activity for almost everyone, the population was necessarily concentrated in the scarce fertile areas: in the coastal plains, estuaries, and river valleys edged by mountains, on isolated

EUROPEAN COUNTRIES TODAY: GREECE

ABOVE: *Navagio beach, on the island of Zakynthos, is famous for its shipwreck, which can be seen on the beach. This beautiful island is situated in the Ionian Sea.*

GREECE'S GEOGRAPHY & LANDSCAPE

ABOVE: *The Corinth Canal is a waterway that connects the Gulf of Corinth with the Saronic Gulf in the Aegean Sea. It cuts through the narrow Isthmus of Corinth and separates the Peloponnese from the Greek mainland.*

plateaux, and on the islands. It is not surprising that there was competition for these areas and that, from time to time, groups of people migrated from less favoured to more favored land, where they formed relatively isolated but close communities. There are no great navigable rivers, and roads have to find their way round mountains. Thus, when incomers brought their stories and their gods to a new area, the stories and the gods were likely, over time, to be assimilated into existing ones, to be given local significance, and to be subjected to local interpretation.

Ancient Greek civilization developed with man's ability to make and use metal. In the Aegean area, the effects of the new technology of the Early

Bronze Age were most obvious at first in the Cycladic Islands, but from about 2500 BEC they seem to have spread throughout the area and reached parts of mainland Greece. Higher civilizations that were both urban and literate had, of course, already come into being by this time in favorable areas, to the east in Mesopotamia—in the fertile plain of the Tigris and the Euphrates—and, slightly later, to the south in Egypt—in the Nile Valley. These cultures were influential in the eastern Mediterranean throughout the Early Bronze Age.

ABOVE: *A view of Chora (Mykonos town) on the island of Mykonos. The island is one of the Cyclades group of islands.*

🇬🇷 **GREECE'S GEOGRAPHY & LANDSCAPE**

Islands

Much of Greece is made up of thousands of islands, forming archipelagos. In fact, approximately six thousand islands surround the mainland; these islands form a fifth of Greece's total land area.

Greece is famous for the clarity of its light and no place is very far from the sea. The islands, therefore, are an integral part of the country's culture and tradition. Greek sovereign land includes islands and islets scattered in the Aegean and Ionian Seas. Only 227 islands are inhabited, the largest of which is Crete, acquired by Greece in 1913, and lies in the southern part of the Aegean Sea.

ABOVE: *The beautiful village of Oia is perched high up on a volcanic outcrop that forms the island of Santorini in the Cyclades group of islands. Santorini is essentially what remains after a volcanic eruption that destroyed the earlier settlements on the island.*

EUROPEAN COUNTRIES TODAY: GREECE

ABOVE: An old street in the town of Chania on the island of Crete. The history of Crete goes back to the seventh millennium BCE, preceding the ancient Minoan civilization by more than four millennia.

Nowadays, the economic and industrial center of Greece is in the capital city Athens, and, therefore, the islands have managed to remain relatively unspoilt and also have retained their traditional cultures and way of life in general. The Greek islands have thousands of miles of coastlines, which include breathtakingly beautiful sandy beaches, pebble beaches, coastal caves, and coastal wetlands.

The Greek islands are rich in unique archeological sites. Some of the most notable are in Crete, Delos, Naxos, Rhodes, and Kos. The islands are also famous for fine cooking where you can find fresh meat, fish, and vegetables, cooked simply and traditionally, in the world-famous Greek style.

GREECE'S GEOGRAPHY & LANDSCAPE

Climate

The surrounding presence of the sea moderates Greece's climate. As a result, it has a temperate climate. The country's summers are hot and dry, and its winters are mild and often wet. The norther portion of the country is somewhat cooler, especially during the winter. Neither season commonly experiences extreme temperatures, the average January temperature being 50 degrees F (10 degrees C) and the average temperature in July being 82 degrees F (28 degrees C). Snow falls in the higher mountains.

Animals and Plants

Greece is able to boast of a huge variety of flora and fauna that live within its borders. Over six thousand species of plants grow in Greece, including more than one hundred different types of orchid. Other plants such as crocuses, irises, lilies, poppies, and a large number of wild herbs also grow there. Native trees include olive, cypress, evergreen oak, juniper, and myrtle.

ABOVE: *Metsovo is a town in the Pindus mountain range in northern Greece. In winter, the town is particularly beautiful when the snow falls.*

EUROPEAN COUNTRIES TODAY: GREECE

Eurasian Lynx

The Eurasian or European lynx is a medium-sized cat native to Europe. It is the third-largest predator after the brown bear and gray wolf. It is the largest of the four lynx species and a strict carnivore, consuming two or three pounds (one or two kg) of meat every day. This extremely efficient hunter uses fine-tuned stealth and pounce techniques to bring down animals four times its size, delivering a fatal bite to the neck or snout of an unsuspecting deer. During winter, its variably patterned coat is long and dense and large fur-covered paws help it move through deep snow. The Eurasian lynx is an endangered species. It can be found in Greece, but in small numbers. Its main threat is hunting and habitat loss.

Source: http://www.bbc.co.uk/nature/life/Eurasian_Lynx

The mountains and the forests are home to animals like deer, badgers, lizards, lynx, and snakes. Several species of bird, especially birds of prey such as eagles and hawks, fly above Greece. Other birds include partridge, pelicans, and pheasants.

Natural Disasters

Unfortunately, Greece is subject to several types of natural disasters. The most dangerous are earthquakes and volcanoes. Earthquakes have been relatively common in Grecian history, since the country is located on a fault line. The most

GREECE'S GEOGRAPHY & LANDSCAPE

recent earthquake occurred in 2017, in Kos, where 150 people were injured.

Volcananic eruptions are other looming natural disasters that threaten Greece and its citizens. They have a long history here. The first recorded eruption of a volcano in what is now Greece was in 258 BCE, more than 2,000 years ago. Besides the fear and destruction these eruptions have caused, they have also played a role in forming many of the islands that surround Greece's mainland.

Environmental Concerns

Greece has had to face numerous threats to its environment but is working hard to counteract some of them. For example, air pollution is an urgent problem in Greece. The rise in industrialization in its cities has led to respiratory problems, damage to ancient Greek artifacts and architecture, and a disruption

ABOVE: *Nisyros is a volcanic island situated in the Dodecanese island group. Volcanic activity has dramatically shaped the topography of the island.*

EUROPEAN COUNTRIES TODAY: GREECE

to the environment. The government is attempting to fight this problem by restricting the number of cars allowed into a city at one time, as well as by promoting the use of cars that pollute less.

Greece's biodiversity is also threatened. Hunting and fishing are popular activities that have damaged the populations of thousands of species on the land and in water. People have often resorted to killing animals such as wolves and bears since they consider them a threat. Unfortunately, this has made these animals endangered. Other endangered species include sea turtles, dolphins, and Mediterranean monk seals, of which there are only several hundred left.

The natural environment is also in danger. Though Greece was once home to vast forested lands, only parts of the north are still forested. Human activities like deforestation and manmade forest fires have brought about the destruction of these natural environments.

Text-Dependent Questions

1. Where are the Pindus Mountains located?

2. How many Greek islands are there?

3. When was the first recorded volcanic erruption in Greece?

Research Project

Write an essay on the flora and fauna of Greece and describe some of the adaptations they have that suit their environment.

Words to Understand

archaeologists: People who study past human life and activities as shown by objects (as pottery, tools, and statues) left by ancient peoples.

prehistoric: Relating to, or existing in the time before people could write.

Roman Empire: The lands and peoples subject to the authority of ancient Rome.

BELOW: The ruin of Athena Pronaia temple is at the ancient site of Delphi. It occupies an impressive area on the southwestern slope of Mount Parnassus. At the center is the Tholos, a circular building that was created between 380 and 360 BCE.

Chapter Two
THE GOVERNMENT & HISTORY OF GREECE

Greece's ancient history is familiar to many students in the Western world, but historians often debate just when the period referred to as "Ancient Greece" began. Some say it began with the first Olympic Games in 776 BCE, and some include the **prehistoric** Minoans and Mycanaeans as part of Ancient Greece. However, Ancient Greece is now usually acknowledged to have begun around 1000 BCE.

Greece's history is important to the history of the world. Greek culture influenced the later **Roman Empire**, which in turn directly affected Western Europe and the Americas. In order to understand Western society's beginnings, it is important to understand Greek society.

Prehistoric Greece

What is now modern-day Greece was originally inhabited by a group of people known as the Minoans. The earliest recorded sign that the Minoans lived on the Balkan Peninsula dates to approximately 3000 BCE. These people

ABOVE: The ruins of the Minoan Palace of Knossos. The palace is the largest Bronze Age archaeological site on Crete. It was the center of the Minoan culture and civilization.

THE GOVERNMENT & HISTORY OF GREECE

Educational Video

Top Five Facts about Ancient Greece.

ABOVE: The Lion Gate guards the main entrance of the Bronze Age citadel of Mycenae in southern Greece. It was erected during the thirteenth century BCE and is named after the relief sculpture of two lionesses or lions in a powerful pose that stands above the gate.

EUROPEAN COUNTRIES TODAY: GREECE

were peace-loving traders who established ties with other civilizations around the world.

Around 1600 BCE, the Minoans were overtaken by a new group, the Mycenaeans. These people brought the beginning of the Bronze Age with them, which lasted until 1100 BCE. Decorative arts flourished, and the stage was set for later mythological writings meant to have taken place during this time. Mysteriously, the Mycenaean civilization was destroyed. Some **archaeologists** believe an invasion by the Dorians, with their superior weapons made of iron, destroyed the Mycenaean civilization.

Ancient Dark Age

Whatever caused the downfall of the Mycenaeans, Greece entered a dark age. Population declined, as did education and the literacy rate. Even the language stopped being written. Cities were looted and destroyed, or abandoned and

Dating Systems and Their Meaning

You might be accustomed to seeing dates expressed with the abbreviations BC or AD, as in the year 1000 BC or the year AD 1900. For centuries, this dating system has been the most common in the Western world. However, since BC and AD are based on Christianity (BC stands for Before Christ and AD stands for anno Domini, Latin for "in the year of our Lord"), many people now prefer to use abbreviations that people from all religions can be comfortable using. The abbreviations BCE (meaning Before Common Era) and CE (meaning Common Era), mark time in the same way (for example, 1000 BC is the same year as 1000 BCE, and AD 1900 is the same year as 1900 CE), but BCE and CE do not have the same religious overtones as BC and AD.

27

The Gods and Myths of Ancient Greece

The gods and myths of Ancient Greece still have a significant place in Western culture. The thunderbolt of Zeus, the trident of the sea-god Poseidon, and the staff of Hermes are still recognizable and evocative images. We speak familiarly of the constellations of Orion, Cassiopeia, and Andromeda. Modern writers can conjure up the futile heroism of war and the destruction of civilizations by mention of Troy. The heroes Heracles and Odysseus still exemplify strength and wily resourcefulness, respectively, and we all know how Freud made use of the Oedipus myth. The stories of the Greek gods and heroes have been retold, reinterpreted, and alluded to in the painting, sculpture, literature, and music of the Western world for centuries.

Myths might be described as traditional tales that have significance for the people they belong to. They are sometimes connected with early religious or social practices or ceremonies; they sometimes attempt to explain the origins of a group of people or celebrate their victory over another group; they are occasionally explanations of natural phenomena or allegories for the

ABOVE: *The Temple of Poseidon (Poiseidon was god of the sea), is situated in Sounion,*

subordination of savage forces to rational order. Above all, they are good stories that give some shape to human experience and help people to talk about why things are as they are.

The origin of the myths is usually unknown and lies in the very distant past, long before the people who told them could read or write. Because they are stories that one generation of people told orally to another, they developed and changed in the telling according to the customs, tastes and needs of the tellers. We know them only in the form they had attained at the moment when they were written down and only in the versions that happen to have survived. The very act of writing the stories, which usually happened long after they had first been told, probably changed them yet again.

The Greek myths developed over a long period, during which a number of different groups of people inhabited the land we now call Greece. The myths include stories that probably originated in Asia, the Middle East and other parts of Europe, and to see why this is so it is necessary to begin with some account of the land, its changing population and the religion that gradually developed there before the eighth century BCE.

never rebuilt. Art such as pottery and jewelry lacked the intricacy of earlier times. The trade that had grown under the Minoans and Mycenaeans died out.

As Greece slowly emerged from this dark period, culture and civilization began to reappear. Toward the end of the Dark Ages, Phoenicians reintroduced writing to the Greeks. Homer then wrote his epics, and other writers recorded the oral history of the time.

Official Ancient Greece: Learning and War

The city-state (the *polis*) rose in significance during the ancient days of Greece. The two most famous were Athens and Sparta, centers of learning and advancement, although there were many other city-states. Many of the writers and philosophers that students learn about today—including Sophocles, Plato, Aristotle, and Democritus—worked during this period.

By no means did peace always remain intact through this age. Wars were often fought between city-states or between Greek alliances and an outside culture. Two of the bigger conflicts were the Persian Wars and the Peloponnesian War, both taking place during the 400s BCE. This last war led to the defeat of Athens and the weakening of Greece. The Thebans, seeing

ABOVE: *Sophocles, playwright.*

ABOVE: *Aristotle, philosopher.*

EUROPEAN COUNTRIES TODAY: GREECE

ABOVE: *Statue of the philosopher Plato. The statue is located outside the Academy of Athens.*

THE GOVERNMENT & HISTORY OF GREECE

Greece's disadvantage, attacked Sparta, which had been victorious in the Peloponnesian War. Philip II of Macedon, father of Alexander the Great, entered this struggle, paving the way for Greece's empire.

Hellenistic Age

The next stage of Greek history is called the Hellenistic period, considered to have begun with the death of Alexander the Great in 323 BCE. Alexander had begun to build an empire, including Greece, which then spread Greek culture to other areas under his rule.

Over the years, city-states such as Athens attempted to revolt against the empire. These attempts earned Greece limited, but valuable, results. Some southern city-states were able to gain a degree of independence from the empire. Several of these formed the Aetolian League. Unfortunately, after starting a revolt against Macedon, which controlled the empire, these city-states lost their freedoms.

Roman Greece

Meanwhile, while Greece was struggling with its own wars, Rome was gaining in power. The Roman Empire eventually annexed Greece in 146 BCE. Roman rule did not generally affect the average Greek. The area's culture was left alone, and local governments were allowed to function as normally as possible. Despite this freedom, Roman rule did have some impact on Greece, and city-states were required to pay tribute to the empire. But Greece even gained from the Romans: all free males in the empire were given the right to vote.

The Byzantine Empire

After the division of the Roman Empire, Greece became part of the Eastern, or Byzantine, Empire. During this period, Greek life followed the ups and downs of the empire as a whole. Orthodox Christianity became an increasing presence, and wars were fought between the Byzantine Empire and outsiders.

During this time, the people of the Balkan Peninsula began to form a firmer idea of Greek identity. Although the area was relatively poor after joining the Byzantine Empire, it gained a more unified Greek way of life, including a common language and religion.

EUROPEAN COUNTRIES TODAY: GREECE

ABOVE: This monument of Alexander the Great is located by the sea in Thessaloniki.

33

THE GOVERNMENT & HISTORY OF GREECE

Ottoman Rule

In 1453 CE, the Byzantine Empire fell to the Ottomans, a Turkish group of people, and the Byzantine period ended. To avoid Ottoman rule, the Greeks took action in the form of migration. Some traveled to western Europe, while others moved from the plains of Greece to the mountains. The Greeks who ended up under Turkish rule resented it. Greeks often became crypto-Christians, or those who practiced Islam but were secretly Christian. Those who actually converted to Islam were sometimes ostracized by other Greeks who believed the new Muslims were abandoning their Greek heritage.

In 1821, the Greeks began to fight for independence, which they gained in 1829. A republic was initially established but became a monarchy in 1833.

ABOVE: *German soldiers raising the German war flag over the Acropolis in 1941.*

EUROPEAN COUNTRIES TODAY: GREECE

ABOVE: Prime Minister Georgios Papandreou and others at the Acropolis after the liberation from the Axis powers in 1944.

Greece Enters the Modern World

During World War I, Greece fought on the side of the Allies against the Central Powers, including Turkey. After the war, Greece was given small amounts of land in return for its help.

In World War II, Greece again sided with the Allied Powers, although it had little to offer with its small number of troops. Italy invaded Greece in 1940, but Greece earned the first Allied victory of WWII when it defeated Italian forces. Eventually, the Axis Powers overwhelmed Greece and occupied the country. Thousands of people were killed, some in concentration camps, others in battle. Jews were especially hunted by the occupying Germans, although the Greek Orthodox Church tried to save many.

The aftermath of WWII did not see much improvement for the Greeks. Greece's economy had been destroyed during the war and occupation. Many

THE GOVERNMENT & HISTORY OF GREECE

Greeks believed it was time for a change in government. A civil war was fought in 1949 between royalists, who supported the king, and communists.

Greece's government during the 1960s and 1970s was anything but stable. In 1967, a coup overthrew the government and set up the Regime of the Colonels, which forced the king into exile. Many believed the United States was involved in this action. An election in 1974 disbanded the monarchy and set up a democratic constitution the following year.

Greece Today

Democracy has continued to thrive in Greece. The country's government consists of the elected president, elected for a five-year term; the 300-member parliament; and the judiciary system. Voting is universal over the age of eighteen.

ABOVE: Greece's prime minister Alexis Tsipras on an official visit to Belgrade, Serbia, in January 2017.

EUROPEAN COUNTRIES TODAY: GREECE

ABOVE: *A Greek athlete in Thessaloniki, carrying the Olympic flame on its journey to the PyeongChang 2018 Winter Olympics.*

THE GOVERNMENT & HISTORY OF GREECE

ABOVE: The Old Royal Palace in Athens was completed in 1843. It has housed the Hellenic Parliament since 1934.

EUROPEAN COUNTRIES TODAY: GREECE

Today, the Greek economy, despite some small improvements, is stagnant. The country still has outstanding economic reforms to initiate and has significant debt problems. There is also uncertainty over its politics. The country joined the European Union (EU) in 1981 and since then has been a major beneficiary of EU aid. Despite continued tourism and the spread of new technology that has brought Greece into the twenty-first century, recent economic events have put a damper on Greece's prosperity and success. Greece is led by Prime Minister Alexis Tsipras, who has been leader of the left wing party Syriza since 2009. Tsipras came to office in 2015 after winning an election. As prime minister, he has overseen negotiations regarding the Greek government-debt crisis, initiated the Greek bailout referendum, and responded to the European migrant crisis.

Text-Dependent Questions

1. Who were the Minoans?

2. What happened to the Mycenaean civilization?

3. Who did Greece side with in WWII?

Research Project

Write a brief report on the Greek Dark Age.

THE GOVERNMENT & HISTORY OF GREECE

The Formation of the European Union (EU)

The EU is a confederation of European nations that continues to grow. As of 2017, there are twenty-eight official members. Several other candidates are also waiting for approval. All countries that enter the EU agree to follow common laws about foreign security policies. They also agree to cooperate on legal matters that go on within the EU. The European Council meets to discuss all international matters and make decisions about them. Each country's own concerns and interests are important, though. And apart from legal and financial issues, the EU tries to uphold values such as peace, human dignity, freedom, and equality.

All member countries remain autonomous. This means that they generally keep their own laws and regulations. The idea for a union among European nations was first mentioned after World War II. The war had devastated much of Europe, both physically and financially. In 1950, the French foreign minister suggested that France and West Germany combine their coal and steel industries under one authority. Both countries would have control over the

ABOVE: *The entrance to the European Union Parliament Building in Brussels.*

EUROPEAN COUNTRIES TODAY: GREECE

MEMBER COUNTRIES

Austria	Greece	Romania
Belgium	Hungary	Slovakia
Bulgaria	Ireland	Slovenia
Croatia	Italy	Spain
Cyprus	Latvia	Sweden
Czech Republic	Lithuania	United Kingdom
Denmark	Luxembourg	*(Brexit: For the time being, the United Kingdom remains a full member of the EU.)*
Estonia	Malta	
Finland	Netherlands	
France	Poland	
Germany	Portugal	

industries. This would help them become more financially stable. It would also make war between the countries much more difficult. The idea was interesting to other European countries as well. In 1951, France, West Germany, Belgium, Luxembourg, the Netherlands, and Italy signed the Treaty of Paris, creating the European Coal and Steel Community. These six countries would become the core of the EU.

In 1957, these same countries signed the Treaties of Rome, creating the European Economic Community. In 1965, the Merger Treaty formed the European Community. Finally, in 1992, the Maastricht Treaty was signed. This treaty defined the European Union. It gave a framework for expanding the EU's political role, particularly in the area of foreign and security policy. It would also replace national currencies with the euro. The next year, the treaty went into effect. At that time, the member countries included the original six plus another six who had joined during the 1970s and '80s.

In the following years, the EU would take more steps to form a single market for its members. This would make joining the union even more advantageous. In addition to enlargement, the EU is steadily becoming more integrated through its own policies for closer cooperation between member states.

Words to Understand

deficit: An excess of expenditure over revenue.

downturn: A period of reduced economic activity.

tax evasion: A willful and especially criminal attempt to evade the imposition or payment of a tax.

BELOW: *The village of Mouzaki, Ilia, in the Peloponnese region. Seasonal farmworkers pick and dry grapes to make raisins.*

Chapter Three
THE GREEK ECONOMY

As in most countries today, Greece's economy has been changing, shifting from agricultureand services to industry. For decades, the country was able to keep up with the changing world and had a stable and prosperous economy, supported by all sectors. Unfortunately, the global financial crisis hit Greece especially hard in 2008, and, since then, Greece has struggled.

ABOVE: *The dockyards of Perama, which is a port city and a suburb of Athens.*

THE GREEK ECONOMY

The Changing Role of Agriculture and Industry

Agriculture has always been an important part of the Greek economy. However, after the mid-1900s, it began to decline because of the rise in industrial activity. While Greece used to rely almost entirely on exporting agricultural products, it now adds industrial goods to its export list. Greece produces such crops as cotton, grapes, olives, tobacco, and vegetables. Sheep and goats are two of its most important livestock outputs.

Greece began to develop its industries after World War II. This was due to foreign aid and supportive government policies. Industry contributes

ABOVE: *Sacks of newly harvested olives. Olives are processed into oil or marinated and then packaged for export all over the world.*

EUROPEAN COUNTRIES TODAY: GREECE

The Economy of Greece

Gross Domestic Product (GDP): US$194.6 billion (2016 est.)
GDP Per Capita: $26,800 (2016 est.)
Industries: tourism, food and tobacco processing, textiles, chemicals, metal products; mining, petroleum
Agriculture: wheat, corn, barley, sugar beet, olives, tomatoes, wine, tobacco, potatoes; beef, dairy products
Export Commodities: food and beverages, manufactured goods, petroleum products, chemicals, textiles
Export Partners: Italy 11.2%, Germany 7.7%, Cyprus 6.4%, Turkey 5.3%, Bulgaria 5.2%, US 4.3%, UK 4.2%, Lebanon 4.1% (2016)
Import Commodities: machinery, transport equipment, fuels, chemicals
Import Partners: Germany 11.1%, Italy 8.8%, China 6.6%, Russia 6.4%, Netherlands 5.5%, Iraq 5.4%, France 4.4%, South Korea 4.1% (2016)
Currency: euro

Source: www.cia.gov 2017

16 percent to Greece's gross domestic product (GDP), second to the service industry. Processed foods, clothing, chemicals, and cement are Greece's primary industries.

Mining is another source of Greece's exports. Bauxite, nickel, iron ore, asbestos, and marble are all found below the earth and mined extensively.

Employers

The government provides many jobs for the Greek people. Since the government owns and runs many institutions, like banks, schools, and

THE GREEK ECONOMY

hospitals, it must employ people to work there. A large percentage of people also work for businesses owned by government banks.

Those not employed by the government often work for themselves. Traditional family businesses are still a big part of the Greek economy, as is self-employment in newer businesses. The entrepreneurial spirit runs high in Greece.

A Country for Tourists

The ancient history and art, as well as the beaches, of Greece have long proved to be attractive to people around the world. Tourism has provided a big boost to the Greek economy during the last few decades and now accounts for a large part of the country's GDP. The service industry, of which tourism is a part, makes up 80 percent of the GDP. Hotels have been

ABOVE: *Alpha Bank is one of the largest banks in Greece.*

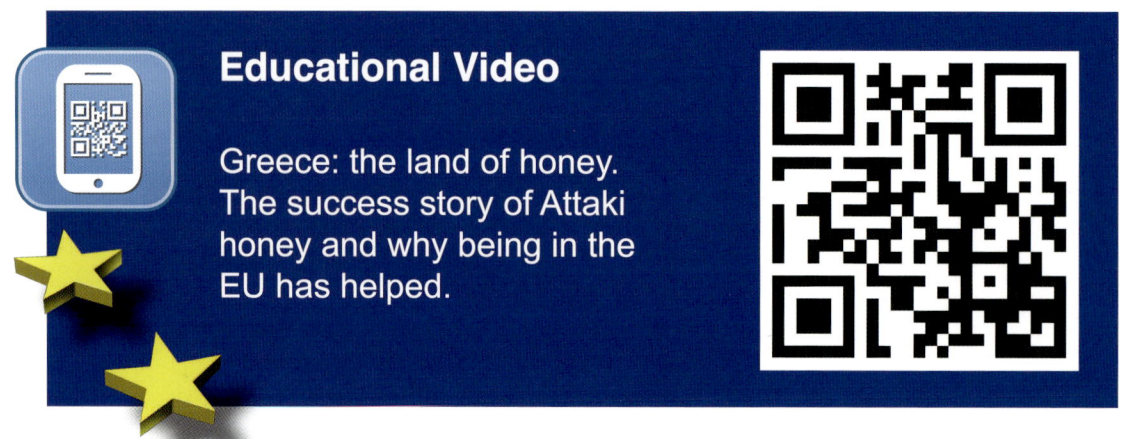

Educational Video

Greece: the land of honey. The success story of Attaki honey and why being in the EU has helped.

EUROPEAN COUNTRIES TODAY: GREECE

ABOVE: *A quarry extracting pumice and obsidian on the island of Gyali in the Dodecanese.*

THE GREEK ECONOMY

built, local arts and crafts sold, and transportation improved to accommodate the growing number of tourists.

Transportation

Greece has a public transportation system that allows visitors and inhabitants to travel around the cities, as well as the whole country. Buses and trains are the two most popular and most extensive systems on land. Athens has a subway system as well. Ferries travel between Greece's many islands.

Greece also has a number of airports, both international and domestic. Olympic Airways and Aegean Airlines offer transportation between Greece's larger cities. International airports are located in Athens and Thessaloniki.

ABOVE: *Greece has long been associated with shipping. Greek ferry companies carry people and goods between its many islands and the mainland.*

EUROPEAN COUNTRIES TODAY: GREECE

ABOVE: Aegean Airlines airplanes lined up at Athens International Airport.

Roads in Greece are usually paved and modern. Six thousand miles (9,656 kilometers) of roads have been classified as national highways, connecting different parts of the country.

Energy

Greece's abundant coal supply provides the country with two-thirds of its energy. Greece also uses oil, but since it does not have this particular resource within its borders, it must import it. Because of its thousands of miles of

49

THE GREEK ECONOMY

ABOVE: *Electricity is produced in a biogas power station. Animal waste is used as a raw material. This plant is in Kolchiko in the north of Greece.*

coastline, Greece is able to exploit the energy from the sea, converting the action of the waves into hydroelectric power, which provides 14 percent of Greece's electricity.

The Debt Crisis

In 2009, Greece's economy took a turn for the worse. There are several reasons for the problems Greece faces today. During the 1990s and 2000s, Greece was doing well financially. Banks and other creditors allowed the Greek government and people to borrow money because it seemed like a safe bet

EUROPEAN COUNTRIES TODAY: GREECE

ABOVE: *Many cities in Greece suffer from pollution, and, as a consequence, Greece is investing in renewable energy. These wind turbines are on the island of Crete.*

51

THE GREEK ECONOMY

that the money would be paid off. However, people spent a lot of money, more than they could afford. The government used loans to build up the country's infrastructure and to improve life. Individuals bought new homes, cars, and other expensive things. In all, spending doubled in the past decade or so.

For a while, everything looked great. Then the world's economy hit a **downturn**. Greece couldn't cope with the new economic problems. The basic problem was that Greece was spending too much money. Its national **deficit** was enormous. By 2016 its deficit was 179 percent of Greece's GDP.

To make matters worse, people hadn't been paying their taxes; many had been practicing **tax evasion**. The government wasn't bringing in enough money to even begin paying off its debts.

ABOVE: Demonstrations in 2016 in Alexandroupolis city center. The demonstration was against the implementation of proposed social security reforms planned by the government, following EU austerity demands.

EUROPEAN COUNTRIES TODAY: GREECE

Prime Minister Alexis Tsipras was elected in 2015. He was a radical anti-austerity, left-wing politician. However, once he assessed the state the country was in, he agreed with the EU to drop key anti-austerity measures and reforms.

Eurozone finance ministers agreed to a number of bailouts to help meet debt repayments. They also agreed on debt relief for Greece, extending the repayment period and capping interest rates. The Greek government had to cut how much it was spending in order to comply with the EU's demands. The cuts included paying government employees less, increasing taxes, raising the retirement age, and reducing pensions. As a consequence, life in Greece has been tough for a long time, and, today, the country is still having economic difficulties. Citizens have had to get used to changes in their lifestyles so that their country can regain its economic health.

Text-Dependent Questions

1. What agricultural crops does Greece produce?

2. How important is tourism to the Greek economy?

3. Name two Greek airlines.

Research Project

Write an essay on Greek agriculture and industry.

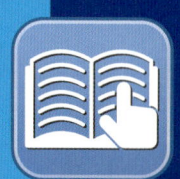

Words to Understand

diversity: The state of having people who are of different races or who have different cultures in a country.

homogeneous: Of the same or a similar kind or nature.

illegal immigrants: Foreign-born residents who have not been naturalized and are still a subject or citizen of a foreign country.

BELOW: Tourists visit the Areopagus, a prominent rock with mythological associations northwest of the Acropolis, Athens.

Chapter Four
CITIZENS OF GREECE: PEOPLE, CUSTOMS & CULTURE

Greece is a very **homogeneous** society; 93 percent of its citizens are ethnic Greeks, with the remaining 7 percent being mainly comprised of Turks and **illegal immigrants**, especially Albanians. As a result, although it lacks diversity, Greece is a unified country whose people share a common culture.

In the 1950s and 1960s, a large number of Greeks left their country for elsewhere in Western Europe. Approximately 10 percent left their homes in Greece in order to escape the troubled times in their country. When times calmed, many returned to their homeland.

ABOVE: During times of economic hardship, some Greeks left home to work abroad. After working away, some returned to their homeland to enjoy their retirement.

CITIZENS OF GREECE: PEOPLE, CUSTOMS & CULTURE

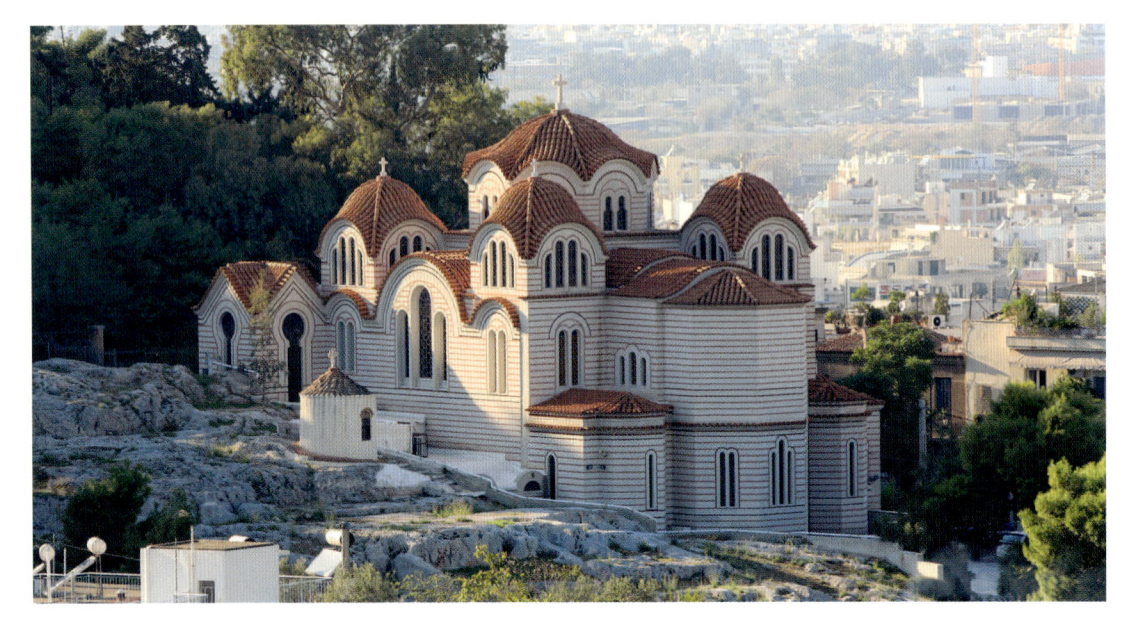

ABOVE: *A Greek Orthodox church near Pnyx in Athens.*

Language

Unlike countries where there is more **diversity** in the population, most Greeks speak the same language. Modern Greek differs from the language of Ancient Greece, but they do share the same alphabet.

In addition to Greek, many people are able to speak German and English. Minorities are sometimes heard speaking Turkish, Macedonian, or Albanian.

Religion

Another unifying force in Greek life is the Greek Orthodox Church. Nearly all of the people living in Greece who are Greek practice this religion. Interestingly, of these people, 10 percent are Old Calendarists, meaning that they use the old Julian calendar instead of the modern Gregorian one. Islam is the next most practiced religion, followed by Roman Catholicism.

Religion plays an integral role in Greek holidays and festivals. Easter is especially important in Greek religious life, as well as the Feast of the Dormition, or Assumption.

EUROPEAN COUNTRIES TODAY: GREECE

Education

Greeks place much importance on education and work hard to provide a good education for students. School attendance is compulsory until age fourteen, when it becomes optional to continue. It is free at all times. Students who continue their education tend to get better jobs in Greece, since many employers require their workers to have had attended school past the age of fourteen.

There are no private universities, so competition for acceptance is tight for those wanting to attend the small number of public universities. Some students attend unofficial private schools that offer higher education or study outside of Greece.

ABOVE: *School children taking part in a Good Friday procession in the old town of Corfu.*

🇬🇷 CITIZENS OF GREECE: PEOPLE, CUSTOMS & CULTURE

Food

From cafés to restaurants, Greeks love to eat their favorite foods out of their own kitchens. Cafés, or *kafeneía*, are popular places to eat pastries or drink a cup of coffee. Once they were open only to men, but that is now changing and women are no longer excluded. Other places, like tavernas, are informal restaurants suitable for eating a full meal.

In restaurants and at home, Greek cuisine shows the influence that Turkey has had on the country. *Souvláki* (meat in pita bread), *tzatzíki* (cucumber and yogurt dip), and *spanakópita* (spinach in phyllo dough) are traditional dishes of Turkish origin. Desserts include *baklavá* and *kataífi*, both made with large amounts of honey, typical in most desserts.

ABOVE: *Stuffed vine leaves (dolmades) are a popular Greek starter. The vine leaves are usually filled with rice, herbs, and meat.*

EUROPEAN COUNTRIES TODAY: GREECE

Baklava
A Greek sweet pastry

Ingredients
14 ounces ground almonds or walnuts
1 cup butter
2 teaspoons cinnamon
1 pinch clove (to taste)
1 pound phyllo pastry dough (sheets)
1 tablespoon lemon juice
2 cups sugar
2 teaspoons vanilla
1 ½ cups water

Directions
Mix the almonds, cinnamon, and cloves. Butter a pan and place 4 buttered sheets of phyllo. Spread a thin layer of the mix then two more sheets of phyllo. Repeat until you have four sheets left, which you use as the top layer. Cut the baklava into slices, all the way to the bottom of the pan. Top with the remaining butter and bake in a 350°F oven for 45 minutes. Mix the sugar, honey, vanilla, lemon juice, and 1 ½ cups of water in a pot and boil for 5 minutes.

Remove any froth off the top and pour over the bakláva. Serve cold.

Tzatziki
An accompaniment or dip

Ingredients
1 large cucumber
4 garlic cloves, crushed
salt and white pepper
squeeze of lemon
10 ounces plain yogurt
1 tablespoon olive oil
1 tablespoon chopped mint

Directions
Peel the cucumber, thinly cut in half lengthways, scoop out and discard the seeds. Chop the flesh finely and place between several layers of kitchen towel. Press hard to remove as much moisture as possible. Transfer the squeezed cucumber into a bowl, add the remaining ingredients, and mix well until blended. Serve chilled with Greek bread or souvlaki.

CITIZENS OF GREECE: PEOPLE, CUSTOMS & CULTURE

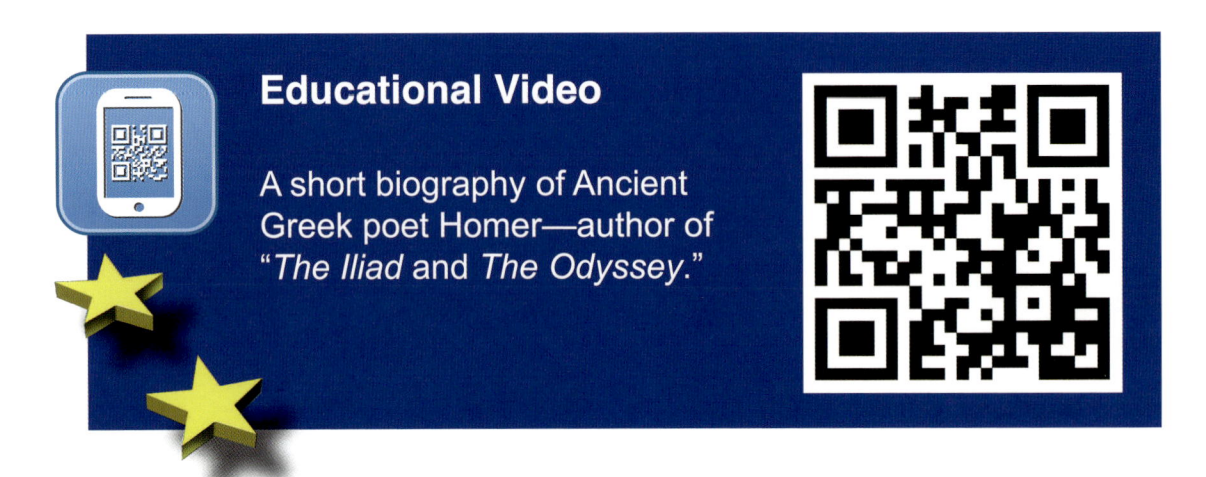

Educational Video

A short biography of Ancient Greek poet Homer—author of "*The Iliad* and *The Odyssey*."

Literature: Past and Present

Many of Greece's writers are famous in the Western world and their works (often referred to as the Classics) are often required reading in school. The most well-known author, Homer, wrote *The Iliad* and *The Odyssey*. Other writers include the poet Sappho, who wrote love poems, and Pausanias, the world's first travel writer.

Although Greek literature is often dominated by the writers of ancient times, the country also boasts well-written modern works. Two Greek poets, Odysseus Elytis and George Seferis, won the Nobel Prize for literature during the twentieth century. Other writers, such as novelist Nikos Kazantzakis, are famous in Greece and becoming better known in other parts of the world.

Sports and the Olympic Games

True to their history of hosting the original Olympic Games, Greeks continue to participate in sports. Soccer (or football, as it's called in Europe) and basketball are popular. The popularity of basketball is very unusual, since it is not so prominent in other European countries.

At the Olympics themselves, Greece has reason to be proud. It hosted the first modern Olympics in 1896 and has since produced many medal-winning athletes. In 2004, Athens again hosted the Olympics, and many stadiums and other accommodations were built especially for the games. Athens now has

EUROPEAN COUNTRIES TODAY: GREECE

state-of-the-art sports facilities, although not necessarily anyone can use them.

Hosting the 2004 Summer Olympics proved to be very costly. Estimates place the cost of the Olympics at $10 or even $15 billion. In fact, the bill, which was footed mostly by the government, added to Greece's current debt crisis.

ABOVE: *A World Cup qualifier match played at the Georgios Karaiskakis Stadium in Piraeus in 2017. Here, the Greek national team is playing Croatia. The Greek player in white is Yannis Gianniotas.*

Theater, Epidaurus

Most Greek theaters were radically changed in later times: the large theater at Epidaurus is the best surviving example that retains its original form, though it has been considerably restored in recent times. It was probably built around 300 BCE and is ascribed to Polykleitos the Younger, who also designed the Tholos, a rare circular building with a cone-shaped roof, in the same area.

Greek theaters were built in the open on a hillside, exploiting the natural slope to provide clear sight lines for a large audience. The audience sat on benches, first wooden, later of stone, in a semicircle. A central block of seats at the front, originally occupied by the priests of Dionysus, whose rites were the starting point for the development of Greek drama, was reserved for important persons, but otherwise seating arrangements seem to have been democratic. Entrance was at one time free, and even after admission charges were introduced the poor did not have to pay. "Tickets" in the form of bronze tags have been found. The performance took place in a large circular, later semicircular, space called the *orchestra*. The altar to Dionysus, once placed in the center, had been removed by the fourth century BCE, though its position can still be seen in the theater at Athens. Behind the *orchestra* was a permanent structure, the *skene*, somewhat resembling a temple façade. It contained the actors' dressing rooms, the few props, and stage machinery, the main item of which was a kind of crane enabling an actor impersonating a god to descend from the sky—the original *deus ex machina*. The theater at Epidaurus had a raised stage with a ramp connecting with ground level. The *orchestra* and the seating have been restored, but not the buildings.

The theater measured about 390 feet (119m) across: though large, it was not unique, having a similar audience capacity to the theater at Syracusa of about 14,000, a figure to make contemporary impresarios blink. Its acoustics are famous, and it is still in use for the annual summer festival of the Greek National Theater.

CITIZENS OF GREECE: PEOPLE, CUSTOMS & CULTURE

Art and Architecture

Throughout the long history of Greece, the art of the area has changed with the age and with the people. Greek art even directly influenced Roman art forms. Sculptures of ancient Greece often depicted human figures or myths. One theme that has remained the same is the Greeks' love of painted pottery, with designs ranging from figures to geometric patterns.

ABOVE: *The Temple of Hephaestus, in Athens, was built in 450 BCE. It is a classical example of Dorian architecture. The temple was dedicated to Hephaestus—the god of metalworking, craftmanship, and fire.*

EUROPEAN COUNTRIES TODAY: GREECE

ABOVE: Adoration of the Magi, *1568, by Doménikos Theotokópoulos, commonly known as El Greco. The artist spent most of his painting career working in Spain and played a large part in the Spanish Renaissance.*

Few examples remain of Ancient Greek architecture; what have survived are mostly temples such as the Temple of Hephaestus and the Parthenon, created by the Greek architect Ictinus. Additionally, many theaters, which were important centers in towns, have survived.

Greek art is not all ancient. More modern artists include El Greco (Doménikos Theotokópoulos) from the island of Crete, who spent most of his

CITIZENS OF GREECE: PEOPLE, CUSTOMS & CULTURE

ABOVE: *A Cretan lyra player, performing on the island of Crete. This stringed instrument is central to the traditional music of Crete and other Greek islands.*

EUROPEAN COUNTRIES TODAY: GREECE

life painting in Spain during the 1500s. Even more recently, artists such as painters Constantine Andreou, Giorgio de Chirico, Jannis Kounellis, and Theodoros Stamos have come out of Greece.

Music and Dance

Traditional forms of music tend to be popular among Greeks, even with the younger generations. One such example is rebetika music, which contains messages about suffering and poverty.

Dances often accompany music, especially at family celebrations and events. The hasapiko, kalamatiano, and tsamiko are all common Greek dances. As in other areas of culture, dances show traditions imported from Turkey.

Text-Dependent Questions

1. Why do Greeks leave home to find work abroad?

2. Who wrote *The Iliad* and *The Odyssey*?

3. Where did El Greco spend much of his life?

Research Project

Learn Greek expressions for simple words such as hello, good day, please, and thank you. Practice them on your friends.

Words to Understand

city-state: An autonomous state consisting of a city and surrounding territory.

industrialization: To build and operate factories and businesses in a city, region, country, etc.

urbanization: The process by which cities grow and become more urban.

BELOW: Athens is one of the world's oldest cities, dating back some 3,400 years. Today, it is the capital and largest city in Greece. Its ancient heritage of the classical era is still evident in the city, represented by numerous ancient monuments and works of art.

Chapter Five
THE FAMOUS CITIES OF GREECE

After World War II, **urbanization**, or the movement of people from rural areas to cities, increased. Today, over 60 percent of Greeks live in urban areas, with one-third of the entire population living in Athens alone.

Athens

Athens has long been an important part of Greece. From starting as a major **city-state**, it has transformed into the country's capital. It was named for Athena, the Greek goddess of wisdom.

The city is the site of many important examples of Greek art and architecture, including the Parthenon, the Acropolis, and the chapel of Ai Giorgis. Its many museums house Greek sculptures and paintings.

Athens is one of the most diverse places in Greece. Many of the country's immigrants, as well as millions of ethnic Greeks, call Athens home. This ethnic diversity, coupled with the culture present in Athens, makes this city a popular destination for tourists. Today, many Greeks work in the tourist industry.

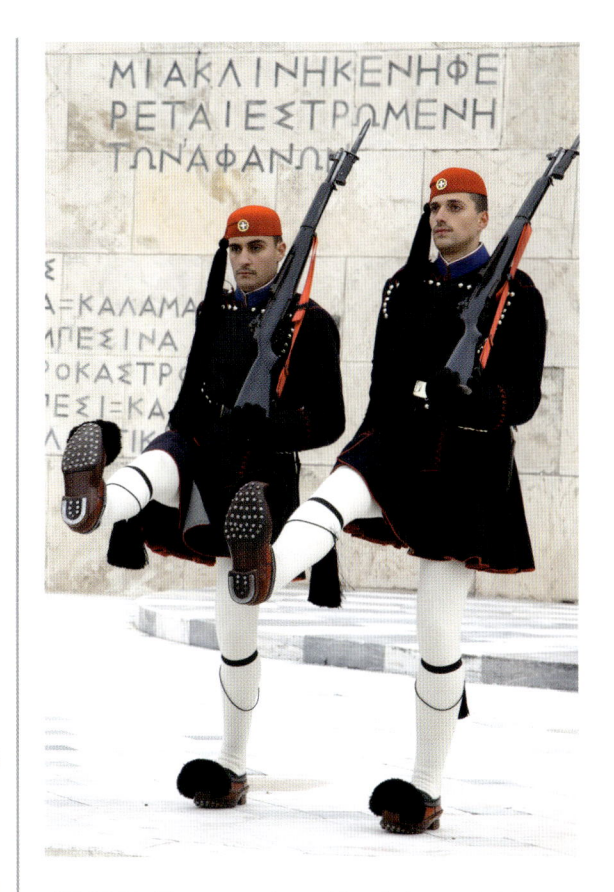

ABOVE: Evzones (presidential guards) in front of the Tomb of the Unknown Soldier outside the Royal Palace, Athens.

THE FAMOUS CITIES OF GREECE

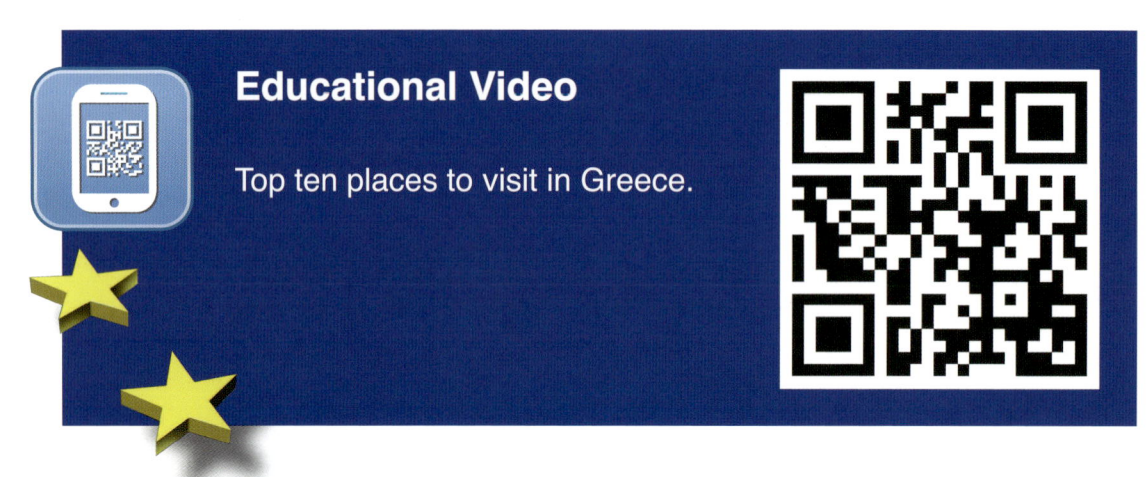

Educational Video

Top ten places to visit in Greece.

ABOVE: *People in a coffee shop in the old town of Plaka near the Acropolis, Athens.*

EUROPEAN COUNTRIES TODAY: GREECE

ABOVE: The archaeological site of Kerameikos, near ancient Agora, in Athens.

Parthenon, Athens

The Parthenon, the shrine built by the Athenians for their patron goddess Athena, is possibly the world's most famous building, and is as near as possible to perfection. It represents the climax of the Doric style, the first of the three Orders, and the one that engaged the Greeks longest and most intensely. Aesthetically, the main criticism of the Doric Order is that it is inclined to be heavy, but the Parthenon, though much the largest temple in Greece, demonstrates by the beauty of its design that this effect is not inevitable. Unusually, it has eight (not six) columns across the porch, and seventeen along each side. The temple stands on the highest point of the Acropolis, and would have been visible from any spot in Periclean Athens. Built in Pentelic marble (the whitest) between 447 and 436 BCE, its architects were Ictinus and Callicrates. The sculpture was by Pericles's friend, the genius Phidias, though naturally many hands were employed. Originally, it contained an image of the goddess 40 feet (12 m) high, by Phidias, in gold and ivory.

At close quarters, the sheer size of the temple is a surprise, being disguised by the perfection of the proportions and subtle devices such as the slight convex curve of the columns (*entasis*) to correct the optical illusion that makes straight columns look concave. Such devices required extraordinary mathematical calculation as well as building skill. The columns are over 34 feet (10 m) high and measure 74 inches (188 cm) in diameter at the base.

   Renaissance drawings show that the Parthenon survived two millennia in good condition, but in 1687 it was partly destroyed by an explosion during a war between Venice and the Ottoman Turks, who had turned it into a mosque and were currently using it as an arsenal. Thereafter, it deteriorated steadily, a process currently accelerating due to atmospheric pollution. In 1801–05 Lord Elgin rescued, though the Greeks say stole, the famous Elgin Marbles (now in the British Museum), including substantial fragments of Phidias's masterpiece, the frieze, which was 524 feet (160 m) long. The frieze was 40 feet (12 m) above the floor and therefore quite hard to see, so, in order to compensate, Phidias designed it with the background to the figures tilted slightly forward.

   The site in currently undergoing a substantial renovation which means that much of it is covered in scaffolding.

THE FAMOUS CITIES OF GREECE

ABOVE: *Aristotelous Square is the main city square of Thessaloniki.*

Thessaloniki

The second-largest city in Greece is the capital of the northern region of Macedonia. Thessaloniki is a very fashionable city, filled with cafés, clubs, and shops. The Thessaloniki Film Festival in the fall is a famous attraction for people all over the world.

EUROPEAN COUNTRIES TODAY: GREECE

ABOVE: *The Roman Rotunda of Galerius (now the Greek Orthodox Church of Agios Georgios), Thessaloniki.*

THE FAMOUS CITIES OF GREECE

The city also has its share of ancient culture, like the tomb of Philip II of Macedon, father of Alexander the Great. There are may Roman and Byzantine ruins as well, reflecting its long history beginning from its foundation in 316 BCE. Newer, but no less important, is the White Tower, the symbol of the city built in the fifteenth century, which sits close to the local university.

ABOVE: *The Church of St. Paul the Apostle, Thessaloniki.*

EUROPEAN COUNTRIES TODAY: GREECE

ABOVE: *The Roman Arch of Galerius in the center of Thessaloniki.*

THE FAMOUS CITIES OF GREECE

Piraeus

Sitting just south of Athens, Piraeus has served as the city's most important port, both in ancient days and in modern times. Its location on the Mediterranean Sea provides ferry access to and from severals islands, including Crete. The port also allow sfor cargo brought into and out of Athens.

Although Piraeus is a city focused on **industrialization**, it still attracts tourists because of its close proximity to Athens and the sea. Its city center, filled with Greek charm, also lures visitors.

ABOVE: *Port of Piraeus and cityscape of Athens, Greece. The port of Piraeus is the largest passenger port in Europe.*

EUROPEAN COUNTRIES TODAY: GREECE

ABOVE: The Market Square in the port of Piraeus, Athens.

THE FAMOUS CITIES OF GREECE

Patras

Patras, or Pátrai, is the largest city on the southern Peloponnesian Peninsula and a major port that provides a gateway from Greece to Italy, and to the many islands surrounding the mainland. Patras's carnival in February is one of the most famous and lively in the country.

The main portion of the city sits below an old castle that dominates the area. Surrounding the castle are restaurants, parks, and shops. Patras also has the Cathedral of St. Andrew, the city's patron saint.

ABOVE: The Patras Carnival is the largest event of its kind in Greece and one of the largest in Europe. The event dates back to the 1870s. It starts on January 17 and lasts up to Clean Monday (Monday of Lent). The carnival is not a single event but a variety of events that include parades, artistic and cultural floats, treasure hunts, and a children's carnival.

EUROPEAN COUNTRIES TODAY: GREECE

ABOVE: *Inside of the castle complex in Patras. The castle was built in the second half of the sixth century CE. Its location gives amazing views of the town, the port, and coast.*

Olympia

Although Olympia is not a major Greek city, it is the namesake of the Olympic Games.

Olympia was the center of the biggest religious festival of Ancient Greece, and of the associated Olympic Games, which, according to tradition, were first held in 776 BCE. The Olympia complex is something of a jumble as town planning did not interest the Greeks; but at its heart was the Temple of Zeus, built between 470 and 456 BCE and at that time the largest building in Greece. The stadium was originally next to it, but was later moved farther east, out of the sanctuary precincts. Events, in which only men took part, though women's races were probably held in the Archaic period, included wrestling, boxing, and chariot racing, as well as track and field events, especially foot races.

THE FAMOUS CITIES OF GREECE

What was then just a slight depression in the ground became the center of intensive German archaeological exploration in 1936, inspired by the Olympic Games in Berlin that year, and continued, after a gap imposed by war, until the 1960s. The end result was the virtual restoration of the stadium to the form it had taken in the fourth century BCE. Races were not run, as now, on an oval track, but in a straight line, so that the main area of the stadium was a narrow rectangle, measuring about 208 x 33 yards (190 x 30 m). The athletes began from a starting gate and ran from end to end. The shortest race was the *stade* (the origin of the word stadium), which was one length. There was also a

ABOVE: *The entrance to the ancient Olympia Stadium, which is situated in the region of Elis on the Peloponnesian Peninsula.*

EUROPEAN COUNTRIES TODAY: GREECE

medium-distance (two lengths) and a long-distance (twenty lengths) race, the athletes rounding a post at each end. Athletes competed naked, but there was also a race for armed men. The excavations revealed the foundations of other structures, including bathhouses with hot-air furnaces to heat the water and provide underfloor heating, the umpires' box about halfway down one side, hand weights held by long-jumpers to gain momentum, and a fourth-century BCE building that appears to have been something like a luxury hotel for the richer competitors. Access to the arena was through a tunnel passing under the sloping bank where spectators sat, on tiers of stone benches.

Today, Olympia is the starting point from which the Olympic torch begins its journey around the world. It is also the headquarters for the modern Olympic Games.

Text-Dependent Questions

1. Who is the Greek goddess of wisdom?

2. Where is the tomb of Philip II of Macedon?

3. When were the Olympic Games first held in Olympia?

Research Project

Write a history of the Olympic Games from the very beginnings to the modern-day event and explain how the games have evolved over the years.

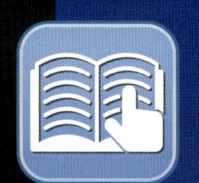

Words to Understand

analysts: People who study or analyze things.

bailout: A rescue from financial distress.

currency: The money that a country uses.

BELOW: Protesters march in a national general strike in Thessaloniki in May 2017. The protest was against austerity measures introduced by the government.

Chapter Six
A BRIGHT FUTURE FOR GREECE

Greece's future is very uncertain. Nobody knows how long it will take the country to recover from its current economic woes. It will be a long struggle, though, with no easy answers, and that struggle will affect plenty of other European countries.

While it is recovering, Greece must rely on help from other members of the EU. Taxpayers from other more stable nations, such as France and Germany, have had to supply the money for Greece's **bailout** loans.

Even if Greece can move past its most immediate problems, the country will still have things to worry about. Investors probably still won't want to put their money into Greece. They will worry that Greece won't be able to pay them back.

The Euro
The problems in Greece could spell out the beginning of the end for the euro. Currently, nineteen members of the EU use the common **currency** of the euro. Altogether, these countries form the Eurozone. The euro was introduced in 1999 and was meant to unify the EU even further. Today, over 338 million people use euros every day.

ABOVE: *Greek and EU flags.*

A BRIGHT FUTURE FOR GREECE

ABOVE: *There are serious questions as to whether Greece can remain in the Eurozone.*

The history of the euro has been challenging for Greece. The Greek government had worked hard to introduce it to the country, forcing the high inflation rate down and increasing taxes. Despite these unpopular policies, Greece was unable to meet the qualifications to adopt the euro. Greece continued working toward acceptance of the euro and finally met the goal set by the EU in 2000. The euro was then put into circulation in 2001.

Some people are afraid that Greece will now leave the Eurozone. It might be better for Greece itself to do that; it could help the country pay off its debts. However, it wouldn't be so good for the rest of the Eurozone. Other EU members are having the same problems as Greece, although on a smaller scale. Portugal and Spain, along with Italy and Ireland, all have debt problems

EUROPEAN COUNTRIES TODAY: GREECE

ABOVE: *Rhodes is very popular with tourists. The landmark of the Suleymaniye Mosque is in the background.*

A BRIGHT FUTURE FOR GREECE

that are being made worse by the global financial crisis. These other countries might decide to do the same thing, and eventually the euro would just collapse.

No one's really sure what's going to happen. While some **analysts** are raising the alarm, others claim that the euro is just fine and that there's nothing to worry about. The EU has so far been committed to keeping the Eurozone intact.

Greece's Future

One major bright spot for Greece is tourism. People still want to visit the country's ancient sites and beautiful coasts. So far, they aren't letting the country's financial problems get in the way.

Tourism is continuing to increase, as foreign visitors pour into Greece. The debt crisis doesn't affect the average tourist, who still has plenty of money to

ABOVE: *Despite its economic problems, Greece is still a stunning country that attracts vast numbers of tourists each year.*

EUROPEAN COUNTRIES TODAY: GREECE

spend on hotels, dinners, boating tours, and other things. Tourists bring in money and make sure that jobs are still available for those who need them. Tourism could help Greece recover more quickly and get back on its feet.

Greece's recovery will be based partly on how the rest of the EU is doing. Other countries are teetering on the edge of their own crises; although, so far, none are as serious as Greece's.

Will Greece be able to repay its loans? Will it leave the euro behind? Will the Greek people continue to lose jobs and security? Only time will tell. And it will depend on the EU's ability to work together to help a member in need. However, some good news—after more than half a decade of gruelling, austerity-driven recession, Greece forecasted economic growth in 2017, in what was its first annual rebound in seven years.

Text-Dependent Questions

1. Which EU nations have helped to bailout Greece?

2. Which other EU countries have similar debt problems to Greece?

3. Why is tourism so important for the Greek economy?

Research Project

Make a list of all the places, seas, and islands you have read about in this book and mark them on a map of Greece.

CHRONOLOGY

3000 BCE	The Minoans arrive in Greece.
1600	Mycenaeans invade Greece; the Bronze Age begins.
1100	The Bronze Age ends.
1100–700	The Dark Age envelops Greece.
776	The first Olympic Games are held.
497–479	The Persian Wars are fought.
461–445	The first Peloponnesian War occurs.
323	Alexander the Great dies.
146	Greece is annexed into the Roman Empire.
395 CE	The Byzantine Empire is formed.
1453	The Byzantine Empire falls to the Ottomans.
1812	The Greeks begin to fight for independence.
1829	The Greeks win their independence from the Turks.
1940	Italy invades Greece.
1949	The Greek civil war is fought.
1974	An election leads to the disbanding of the monarchy.
1975	A democratic constitution goes into effect.
1981	Greece joins the EU.
2001	Greece adopts the euro.
2004	Greece hosts the Summer Olympics.
2008	The world faces a global recession.
2009	Greece's economy goes into recession. George Papandreou becomes prime minister.
2011	Lucas Papademos becomes prime minister.
return	Eurozone leaders agree a 50 percent debt write-off for Greece in for further austerity measures.
2014	Eurozone finance ministers say they'll release more than €8 billion of further bailout funds to Greece.
2016	Alexis Tsipras of Syriza becomes prime minister after winning parliamentary elections.
	Eurozone agrees to unlock a further €10.3 billion in loans. They also agree on debt relief, extending the repayment period and capping interest rates.

FURTHER READING & INTERNET RESOURCES

Further Reading

Brewer, Stephen. *Frommer's Athens and the Greek Islands.* New York: FrommerMedia, 2016.

McCormick, John. *Understanding the European Union: A Concise Introduction*. London: Palgrave Macmillan, 2017.

Mason, David S. *A Concise History of Modern Europe: Liberty, Equality, Solidarity.* London: Rowman & Littlefield, 2015.

Miller, Korina. Armstrong, Kate. Averbuck, Alexis. Clark, Michael S. Kaminski, Anna. Maric, Vesna. McLachlan, Craig. O'Neill, Zora. Ragozin, Leonid. *Lonely Planet Greece (Travel Guide)*. London: Lonely Planet Publications, 2018.

Internet Resources

Greece Travel Information and Travel Guide.
https://www.lonelyplanet.com/greece

Visit Greece.
http://www.visitgreece.gr

Greece: Country Profile
http://www.bbc.co.uk/news/world-europe-17372520

Greece: CIA World Factbook
https://www.cia.gov/library/publications/the-world-factbook/geos/gr.html

The Official Website of the European Union
europa.eu/index_en.htm

Publisher's note:
The websites listed on this page were active at the time of publication. The publisher is not responsible for websites that have changed their addresses or discontinued operation since the date of publication. The publisher will review and update the website list upon each reprint.

INDEX

A

Academy of Athens, 31
Acropolis, 34, 35, 54, 69, 72
AD (anno Domini), 27
Adoration of the Magi (Theotokópoulos), 65
Aegean
    Airlines, 48, 49
    Sea, 7, 8, 11, 13, 16, 18
Aetolian League, 32
Agora, 71
Agriculture, 14, 43
    changing role of, 44–45
Ai Giorgis, 69
Airports, 48
Albania, 7
Albanian language, 56
Albanians, 55
Alexander the Great, 32, 33, 76
Alexandroupolis, 52
Allied Powers, 35
Alpha Bank, 46
Ancient
    Dark Age, 27, 30
    Greece, 25, 30–32, 81
Andreou, Constantine, 67
Andromeda, 28
Animals, 21
    endangered, 23
Archipelagos, 18
Architecture, 65, 67
Area, 7, 11
Areopagus, 54
Aristotelous Square, 74
Aristotle, 30
Art, 30, 46, 64, 65–67
Asia Minor, 13
Assumption, 56
Athena, 69, 72
    Pronaia, 24
Athens, 19, 30, 32, 38, 43, 48, 54, 56, 60, 64, 68, 69–73, 78, 79
    International Airport, 49
    theater, 63
Attaki honey, 46
Attica Peninsula, 28
Axis powers, 35

B

Bailout, 85
Baklavá, 58, 59
Balkan Peninsula, 11, 25, 32
Basketball, 60
BC (Before Christ), 27
BCE (Before the Common Era), 27
Belgium, 41
Belgrade, 36
Berlin, 82
Biodiversity, 23
Birth rate, 9
Borders, 7
British Museum, 73
Bronze Age, 25, 26, 27
Brussels, 40
Bulgaria, 7, 45
Byzantine Empire, 32

C

Cafés *(kafeneías)*, 58
Callicrates, 72
Capital, 19, 69
Cassiopeia, 28
Cathedral of St. Andrew, 80
CE (Common Era), 27
Chania, 19
China, 45
Chirico, Giorgio de, 67
Chora (Mykonos town), 17
Christianity, 8, 34
    Orthodox, 32
Church of
    Agios Georgios, 75
    St. Paul the Apostle, 76
Citadel of Mycenae, 26
Cities, 69–83
City-states (polis), 11, 30, 69
    revolts, 32
    and Roman Empire, 32
Civilization, spread of, 16–17
Civil war, 36
Classics, 60
Clean Monday, 80
Climate, 7, 8, 20
Coal, 49
Coastline, 11, 14, 19
Corfu, 57
Corinth Canal, 16
Crete, 18, 19, 25, 51, 65, 66, 78
Crypto-Christians, 34
Currency, 41, 45, 85–86
Cyclades Islands, 17, 18
Cyprus, 45

D

Dating systems, 27
Death rate, 9
Delos, 19
Delphi, 24
Democritus, 30
Demonstrations, 52
Deus ex machina, 63
Dionysus, 62, 63
Diversity, 14, 55
Dodecanese islands, 13, 22, 47
Dolmades, 58
Dorian architecture, 64
Dorians, 27
Doric style, 72
Drama, 62

92

INDEX

E

Early Bronze Age, 16–17
Earthquakes, 7, 21–22
Easter, 56
Economy, 39, 43–53, 85–86, 88, 89
    bailout, 39
    debt crisis, 39, 50, 52–53, 61
    deficit, 52
    post-war, 35–36
Education, 27, 57
Egypt, 13
Electricity, 50
Elevation, 7
Elgin
    Lord, 73
    Marbles, 73
Elis, 82
Elytis, Odysseus, 60
Employers, 45–46
Energy, 49–50
    renewable, 51
English language, 9, 56
Environment, 22–23
Epidaurus, 62
    theater, 62–63
Ethnic groups, 9, 55
Euphrates river, 17
Eurasian lynx, 21
Euro, 41, 45, 85–86, 89
European
    Coal and Steel Community, 41
    Community, 41
    Council, 40
    Economic Community, 41
European Union (EU), 39, 85
    austerity measures, 52, 53
    autonomy, 40
    flag, 85
    formation, 40–41
    members, 40, 41
    Parliament Building, 40
    single market, 41
    values, 40
Eurozone, 86
Evzones (presidential guards), 69
Exports, 45

F

Feast of Dormition (Assumption), 56
Fertility rate, 9
Flag, 8, 85
Food, 19, 58–59
Football, 60
Forests, 23
France, 40, 41, 45
French language, 9
Freud, 28
Frieze, 73
Future, 85–89

G

Geography, 7
    and landscape, 11–23
Georgios Karaisakakis Stadium, 61
German language, 56
Germany, 34, 35, 45
Gianniotas, Yannis, 61
Gods, 28–29
Good Friday, 57
Government, 25–41
Grapes, 42
Greco, El. *See* Theotokópoulos, Doménikos (El Greco)
Greek
    language, 9
    National Theater, 63
    Orthodox Church, 35, 56
    Orthodoxy, 9
Gregorian calendar, 56
Gross domestic product (GDP), 45, 46, 52
    per capita, 45
Gulf of Corinth, 16
Gyali, 47

H

Hasapiko, 67
Hazards, 7
Hellenic
    Parliament, 38
    Republic, 11
Hellenistic Age, 32
Hephaestus, 64
Heracles, 28
Hermes, 28
History, 25–41, 46
Homer, 14, 30

I

Ictinus, 65, 72
Ilia, 42
Iliad, The, 60
Immigration, 39, 69
    illegal, 55
Imports, 45
Independence, 34
Industrialization, 78
Industry, 44–45
Infant mortality rate, 9
Ionian Sea, 11, 15, 18
Iraq, 45
Ireland, 86
Islam, 9, 34, 56
Islands, 18–19

INDEX

Isthmus of Corinth, 16
Italy, 35, 41, 45, 80, 86

J

Jews, 35
Judiciary system, 36
Julian calendar, 56

K

Kalamatiano, 67
Kataífi, 58
Kazantzakis, Nikos, 60
Kerameikos, 71
Kolchiko, 50
Kos, 19, 22
Kounellis, Jannis, 67

L

Language, 9, 32, 56
    alphabet, 56
Larissa, 8
Lebanon, 45
Libya, 13
Life expectancy, 9
Light, clarity of, 18
Lion Gate, 26
Literacy rate, 9, 27
Literature, 60
Localism, 14
Location, 7
Luxembourg, 41
Lyra, 66

M

Maastricht Treaty, 41
Macedon, 32
Macedonia, 7, 74
Macedonian language, 56
Map, 6, 10
Maritime civilizations, 14

Mediterranean Sea, 7, 8, 11, 13, 14, 78
Merger Treaty, 41
Mesopotamia, 17
Metal, 16
Metsovo, 20
Migration rate, 9
Mining, 45
Minoan civilization, 19, 25, 27, 30
Monarchy, 34, 36
Mount
    Olympus, 7, 11, 12
    Parnassus, 24
Mountains, 7, 11, 12, 13, 14, 16, 24
Mouzaki, 42
Music and dance, 67
Mycanaeans, 25, 27, 30
Mykonose, 17
Mythology, 12, 13, 28–29

Natural disasters, 21–22
Navagio beach, 15
Naxos, 19
Netherlands, 41, 45
Nile Valley, 17
Nisyros, 22
Nobel Prize, 60

Odysseus, 28
Odyssey, The, 11, 60
Oedipus, 28
Oia, 18
Oil, 49
Old
    Calendarists, 56
    Royal Palace, 38
Olive tree, 14, 44
Olympia, 81–83
    Stadium, 81–82
Olympic
    Airways, 48
    Games, 37, 60, 61, 81–83
Orchestra, 63
Orders, 72
Orion, 28
Ottoman
    Rule, 34
    Turks, 73

P

Palace of Knossos, 25
Papandreou, Georgios, 35
Parliament, 36
Parthenon, 65, 69, 72–73
Patras (Pátrai), 80
    Carnival, 80
    castle, 81
Pausanias, 60
Peloponnese, 16
    region, 42
Peloponnesian
    Peninsula, 11, 82
    War, 30, 32
People, 9, 55–67
Perama, 43
Pericles, 72
Persian Wars, 30
Phidias, 72
Philip II of Macedon, 32, 76
Philosophy, 30
Phoenicians, 30
Pindus Mountains, 11, 20
Piraeus, 61, 78, 79
Plaka, 70
Plants, 20–21
Plato, 30, 31
Pnyx, 56
Pollution, 22–23, 51
Polykleitos the Younger, 62
Population, 9, 27
    age, 9

INDEX

growth rate, 9
Portugal, 86
Poseidon, 28
Prehistory, 25, 27
President, 36
Prime minister, 35, 36, 39, 53

Q
Quarry, 47

R
Rebetika music, 67
Recipes, 59
Regime of the Colonels, 36
Religion, 9, 56
Republic, 34
Rhodes, 19, 87
Rivers, 16
Roads, 49
Roman
    Arch of Galerius, 77
    Catholicism, 56
    Greece, 32
    Rotunda of Galerius, 75
Roman Empire, 25, 32
    annexation of Greece, 32
Romans, 8
Royal Palace, 69
Russia, 45

S
Santorini, 18
Sappho, 60
Saronic Gulf, 16
Seferis, George, 60
Serbia, 36
Shipping, 48
Shipwreck, 15
Soccer, 60

Socrates, 11
Sophocles, 30
Sounion, 28
South Korea, 45
Souvláki, 58
Spain, 65, 86
Spanakópita, 58
Spanish Renaissance, 65
Sparta, 30, 32
Sports, 60–61
Stamos, Theodoros, 67
Strike, 84
Suleymaniye Mosque, 87
Symi, 13
Syracusa, 63
Syriza, 39

T
Tavernas, 58
Tax evasion, 52
Technology, 11
Temple of
    Hephaestus, 64, 65
    Poseidon, 28
    Zeus, 81
Terrain, 7, 11–17
Thebans, 30, 32
Theotokópoulos, Doménikos (El Greco), 65
Thessaloniki, 33, 37, 48, 74–77, 84
    Film Festival, 74
Tholos, 24
Tigris river, 17
Tomb of the Unknown Soldier, 69
Tourism, 39, 46, 48, 69, 88–89
Transportation, 48–49
Treaties of Rome, 41
Treaty of Paris, 41
Troy, 28

Tsamiko, 67
Tsipras, Alexis, 36, 39, 53
Turkey, 7, 45, 67
Turkish language, 56
Turks, 8, 55
Tzatzíki, 58, 59

U
United
    Kingdom, 45
    States, 36, 45
Universities, 57
Urbanization, 69

V
Venice, 73
Volcanoes, 22
Voting, 32, 36

W
West Germany, 40, 41
White Tower, 76
Wind turbines, 51
World Cup, 61
World War
    I, 35
    II, 35, 40, 44
Writing, 27, 30

Z
Zakynthos, 15
Zeus, 28

Picture Credits

All images in this book are in the public domain or have been supplied under license by © Shutterstock.com. The publisher credits the following images as follows: Page 8: Ruben M. Ramos, page 25: Dziewul, page 33: Fritz16, page 36: Golden Brown, page 37: Giannis Papanikos, page 38, 54: Lucian Milasan, page 43, 50, 84: Ververidis Vasilis, page 48: Ales Munt, page 52: 1000 Words, page 52: Blackboard1965, page 53: StockStudio, page 57: Dimitrina Lavchieva, page 61: Kostas Kontisaftikis, page 69: Dmytro Shapoval, page 70, 71, 81: Milan Gonda, page 77: Hdessislava, page 78, 87: Littleaom, page 79: Salvador Aznar, page 80: dwpotos.

To the best knowledge of the publisher, all images not specifically credited are in the public domain. If any image has been inadvertently uncredited, please notify the publisher, so that credit can be given in future printings.

Picture Credits

Page 12 Geography Now!: http://x-qr.net/1DSb
page 26 WatchMojo.com: http://x-qr.net/1Dv3
page 46 euronnews: http://x-qr.net/1DgU
page 60 CloudBiography: http://x-qr.net/1DKj
page 70 Davidsbeenhere: http://x-qr.net/1HkK

Author

Dominic J. Ainsley is a freelance writer on history, geography, and the arts and the author of many books on travel. His passion for traveling dates from when he visited Europe at the age of ten with his parents. Today, Dominic travels the world for work and pleasure, documenting his experiences and encounters as he goes. He lives in the south of England in the United Kingdom with his wife and two children.